The Gifts of

Mother Earth

*Dedicated to my husband, Steve and my son,
Alexander with all my love — E.A.*

An imprint of JVT

Text copyright © 2019 by Erika Abonyi
Illustrations copyright © 2019 by Minji Kim

All rights reserved, including the right of reproduction in whole or in part in any form.

JVT is a trademark of JVT, Inc. and related logo is a registered trademark of JVT, Inc.

For information about special discounts for bulk purchases, please contact at
business@thegiftsofmotherearth.com or visit our website
at thegiftsofmotherearth.com

The illustrations for this book were rendered in watercolor.

The text of this book was set in Diotima

Summary: Children get together to connect and celebrate the
beauty and generosity of Mother Earth through
the ever-changing seasons.

Library of Congress Control Number 2019921046
ISBN 978-0-578-62942-1 (hc)

Manufactured in China

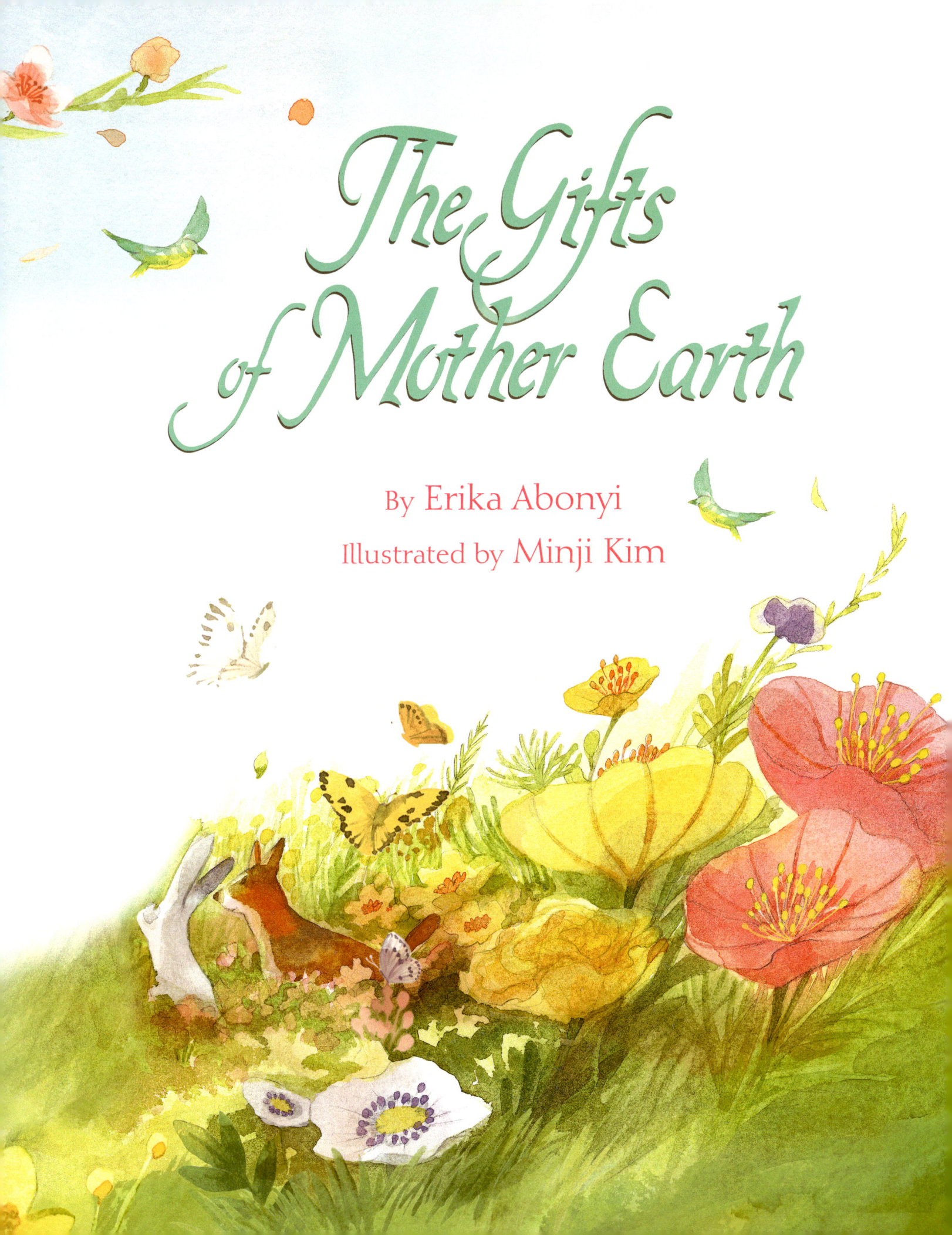

The Gifts of Mother Earth

By Erika Abonyi

Illustrated by Minji Kim

One bright spring day, Alex and his friends—Lyra, Bella and Max—had an idea. They decided to plant a seed in the garden. Their mission was to work closely with Mother Earth to make the world a more beautiful place. The children buried the seed in the ground, poured plenty of water on it and then stepped back. They loved the feel of the earth, and their hearts were full of joy.

After planting the seed, the children used a stick to draw a circle around it and then sang a happy song. They asked Mother Earth to kindly awaken this little seed, bring it to life and bless it with love and care. They knew Mother Earth could be trusted to do this, and their hearts felt kindness and love.

It soon started to rain and the thirsty ground drank the water and fed the little seed. After a few days, a little seedling peeked out above the ground and quickly sprang up to become a small green plant. Then, as if by magic, it grew into a beautiful cherry tree. The children were happy as they danced in the rain. They felt the power of Mother Earth, and their hearts were full of joy.

The sun was shining bright and warm and the raindrops on the leaves sparkled like crystals. A rainbow with seven different colors appeared in the sky, looking like a magical bridge between Sky and Earth. The children were excited and imagined sliding down the rainbow as if in a dream. They saw how miraculous Mother Earth is, and they were elated.

Blooms began to appear on the cherry tree and a lovely smell filled the air. Colorful flowers filled every corner of the garden. The children had fun blowing fluffy dandelion puffs into the air and watching the little parachutes fly. They made crowns from daisies and poppies and pretended to be flower fairies. They enjoyed the beauty and smell of Mother Earth's creations, and their hearts were full of joy.

A flock of birds settled high on the cherry tree's branches and sang cheerful melodies. The hard-working honey bees buzzed around the tree and collected nectar from the flowers. The world hummed with the life and music from many of Mother Earth's creatures. Alex and his friends watched the birds. They tried to name them by their songs and mimic the drumbeats of woodpeckers and the laughing of owls. They could hear the sounds of Mother Earth rejoicing, and their hearts felt the rhythm of Nature.

One summer day, the tree began to grow fruit. Alex, Lyra, Bella and Max picked the sweet cherries from the tree. The plump fruit tasted juicy and delicious and was also healthy to eat. The children played silly games and laughed while hanging cherries on their

ears. They gave thanks to Mother Earth for the journey of life, from seed to cherry tree. They sang songs to praise Mother Earth for her goodness and to thank her for sharing her gifts with them. They were grateful and, in their hearts, felt blessed.

Mother Earth sent a fairy to protect the tree from wind and storms. The fairy became the guardian of the cherry tree. She flittered near the tree and protected it from harm. The tree grew wide and stood tall. The children watched Mother Earth protect Her creation. They felt safe, and their hearts were full of joy.

Alex's grandma came to the garden to pick some cherries from the tree. She baked a cherry pie and the children enjoyed sharing it with each other. They told Grandma about the journey of the little seed and celebrated the result of their work. The children appreciated the lesson that Mother Earth had taught them, and were thankful for her creations.

Fall came early and the tree became a home for squirrels; they collected seeds and acorns and stored them in a hole in the trunk of the tree so they would have food to last through the winter. The squirrels hopped from branch to branch, searching for more food and spreading seeds for future trees.

The children watched the leaves fall to the ground and tried to catch them and count them. They became aware that everything has a purpose in life. They saw Mother Earth's creatures come together with love, and their hearts were full of joy.

When winter came, snow fell from the sky and the snowflakes carpeted the bare tree branches. The fairy proudly guarded the tree. She reached out to the shiny stars and put them on the tree like garland lights that brightened up the darkness. Tiny sparkle lights were floating in the air like fireflies and the children tried to grab them and hold them in their hands. They saw the light of Mother Earth, and their hearts sparkled with happiness.

Then spring came again and the tree was strong. Its branches, filled with new life, reached high into the sky. The tree's children circled around. Their single seed had become an orchard full of trees! The blossoms were dancing in the air, landing on the children like a thousand butterflies. Some flowers traveled far behind the orchard, creating new cherry trees that were scattered all over the world.

The children rejoiced in the loving nature of Mother Earth. They were delighted to see how her enormous power and nurturing had replenished the earth with new life. They felt hope and trust. Their hearts were full of joy and love.

Thank you, Mother Earth.

Let this story take you along on a magical journey—to a place where everything is possible. It is a land where Mother Earth is living and dreaming, and waiting for you to connect with her to experience the wonders of nature.

Close your eyes and feel what it's like to walk through the flower garden with the children. Take a deep breath and inhale the scent of the flowers. Listen to the songs of the birds. Let Mother Earth touch your heart. She is gentle and loving, so take care of her and protect her. She will gift you with endless beauty.